In Grateful Praise

Down-to-Earth
Prayers of Praise and Thanksgiving

Nick Fawcett

IN GRATEFUL PRAISE
Down-to-Earth Prayers of Praise and Thanksgiving

Copyright © 2007 Nick Fawcett
Original edition published in English under the title IN GRATEFUL PRAISE by Kevin Mayhew Ltd, Buxhall, England.
This edition copyright © Fortress Press 2019

All rights reserved. Except for brief quotations in critical articles or reviews, no part of this book may be reproduced in any manner without prior written permission from the publisher. Email copyright@augsburgfortress.org or write to Permissions, Fortress Press, PO Box 1209, Minneapolis, MN 55440-1209.

The prayers in this book previously appeared in *Touching Down, Heaven Touching Earth, Touched by His Hand,* and *Touching the Seasons.*

Cover image: Cover art from book interior
Cover design: Tory Herman

Print ISBN: 978-1-5064-5931-8

Contents

- 4 Introduction
- 5 The Restored Building
- 6 The Contract
- 7 The Discarded Diary
- 8 The Royal Visit
- 9 The Frost
- 10 The 3-D Glasses
- 11 The Sea Wall
- 12 The Tapestry
- 13 The "Free" Gift
- 14 The Honors List
- 15 The Dinosaur Bones
- 16 The Surveillance Cameras
- 17 The Recorder Player
- 18 The Paint Palette
- 19 The Tennis Court
- 20 The Pricked Finger
- 21 The Ream of Paper
- 22 The Shopping Cart
- 23 The Hairdresser
- 24 The Space Probe
- 25 The Zoo
- 26 The Sunglasses
- 27 The School Run
- 28 The River
- 29 The Symphony
- 30 The Fountain
- 31 The Dawn Chorus
- 32 The Cockerel

Introduction

"Praise, my soul, the King of heaven"—so begins one of our most celebrated hymns—and this book aims to help you do just that. But where, you may ask, should we start and what words ought we to use? A common assumption is that we must focus on God, but that's easier said than done, for God, by definition, is greater than anything we could quite imagine, beyond words or human fathoming. Here, then, I suggest an alternative approach, exploring how praise can well up during the course of daily life, inspired by the seemingly ordinary things of life, whether the beauty of nature, our everyday relationships, or the unfolding of events. Look at the world more carefully and we will not only hear God speaking but find inspiration for our response; all kinds of things can not only speak of God but also lead naturally into prayer.

The prayers in this book, all drawn from four of my recent publications, reflect everyday moments that led me to worship: simple things such as the sight of parents taking their children to school, or even the sharp stab of a needle pricking my finger. Each pointed beyond itself, inspiring praise and thanksgiving. I offer them in the hope that they may inspire you in turn, opening up new dimensions of prayer in your personal response to God.

Nick Fawcett

The Restored Building

It had cost a fortune,
involving innumerable appeals
and funding applications,
and there had been plenty to question the wisdom
of continuing,
convinced the money could have been
spent better elsewhere;
but at last the project was complete
and the building restored to its former glory.
As the crowds filed through,
marveling at its splendor,
all the time and effort seemed more than worth it,
a small price for such a spectacular jewel.

Remind me, Lord, of what it cost you
to restore your broken world,
the price you so freely paid to make us whole.
Remind me of the immensity of your love,
the awesome sacrifice
through which you have made all things new.
I can never repay such goodness,
whatever I offer in return,
but I give you my praise
in grateful thanks
and joyful worship.
Amen.

The Contract

I'd thought I was covered,
the contract protecting me in law,
but as I waded through the fine print
I realized otherwise,
the meaning of complex clauses,
barely understood at the time,
now becoming clear,
invalidating the policy.

Thank you, Lord,
for the contract you have made in Christ,
the new covenant sealed by his death and resurrection,
offering new life and love to all.
Thank you that all it asks for is a response in faith—
no signing on the dotted line
or agreement to complex formulas,
but a simple act of commitment.
Above all, thank you for honoring your pledge,
keeping to your side of the bargain,
even though I repeatedly renege on mine.
Amen.

The Discarded Diary

It was strange, thumbing through it,
for scribbled notes that had spoken of the future
spoke now of the past,
and occasions once keenly anticipated
were now barely remembered,
each part of my past instead of my future,
over and done with, for better or worse.

Thank you, Lord, that in pleasure and pain,
triumph and tragedy,
hope and fear,
health and sickness,
you've been with me across another year,
leading me safely through its ups and downs,
highs and lows.
Teach me, recalling your faithful guidance,
to trust you for all that lies ahead,
knowing that you alone will be the same,
yesterday, today, and tomorrow.
Amen.

The Royal Visit

They lined the streets in their thousands,
cramming into every available space,
pushing, shoving, and straining their necks
to get a sight of the royal procession.
No more than that—
just a fleeting glimpse—
but it was enough to send them home happy,
buzzing with excitement,
for they had seen the Queen,
stood in her presence as she passed briefly by.

Give me, Lord, a similar sense of wonder
in the presence of Christ,
an appreciation of the privilege I have,
day after day,
moment by moment,
of knowing the one who is not just royalty
but the King of kings and Lord of lords,
greater than words can express
or the mind comprehend.
Teach me to make time for him,
not as an extra or afterthought
but as my greatest joy and first priority,
offering him my grateful praise and thankful service.
Amen.

The Frost

It lay thick on the ground,
holding the world in its icy grip—
soil rock hard,
leaves scorched,
buds nipped,
water turned to ice—
yet already new growth was stirring,
bulbs swelling,
snowdrops lifting their dainty heads,
and winter shrubs blossoming in joyful defiance.

Remind me, Lord,
that even in the darkest days of life
and the bleak chill of death,
you are there,
bringing new beginnings.
For your life-giving power,
beyond containment,
receive my praise.
Amen.

The 3-D Glasses

They made such a difference,
giving me a sense of being there,
involved in the action—
for they opened up new dimensions,
giving a fresh perspective on all,
what previously I'd seen in part
now revealed in full.

Help me to see *you* like that, Lord:
in all your glory
rather than tied down by my limited vision.
Help me to glimpse you as Father—
providing,
guiding,
caring for me each day;
to see you as Son—
sharing my humanity
and walking this earth;
to experience you as Spirit—
alive within,
prompting, comforting,
teaching, and equipping.
Give me a fuller picture of who and what you are,
and an awareness that no dimension or measure
can finally contain the wonder of it all.
Amen.

The Sea Wall

It had taken a pounding,
day after day,
year after year,
the mighty sea relentlessly renewing its attack
as wave after wave hurled itself against the wall
and exploded in a cloud of spray.
Yet still it stood,
solid and defiant,
a massive bulwark guarding the town beyond.

Thank you, Lord, for guarding me,
faithfully providing shelter and protection
when storms brew
and waves threaten to sweep me away.
Thank you for the strength of your love
and certainty of your promise,
the knowledge that though all else may pass away
your goodness will continue,
solid and secure in an ever-changing universe.
Whatever I face, I will not fear,
for you are with me,
the same yesterday, today, and forever.
Amen.

The Tapestry

They were just a jumble of threads—
no pattern to them,
no order,
no anything—
but, having sketched out her design,
she painstakingly wove them together,
creating a thing of beauty,
a unique and unforgettable work of art.

Thank you, Lord, for your creation:
the beauty of this world and wonder of the universe.
Thank you for so much that speaks of your purpose,
causing me to catch my breath in awe and wonder.
For the work of your hands
and all it reveals of your love,
receive my praise.
Amen.

The "Free" Gift

"Congratulations!" it said.
"You have won our bumper prize:
the holiday of a lifetime,
yours absolutely free!"
But it wasn't free,
nowhere near it,
for concealed in the small print,
tucked neatly out of view,
lay a host of hidden costs—
the amount I'd eventually pay
far greater than any "gift" I'd receive.

Thank you, Lord, that your gifts are truly free:
your love, mercy, joy, and peace,
blessings too many to number
offered without strings attached.
Thank you for paying the price of these yourself,
sharing our flesh,
bearing our pain,
and dying our death,
so that we might receive life,
now and for all eternity,
a prize indeed too special to miss.
Amen.

The Honors List

They were suddenly elevated in the public eye,
no longer simply Mr. or Mrs.
but Sir, Lord, the honorable and the like—
their names exalted,
achievements recognized,
contributions duly acknowledged.
And why not?—
for they deserved acclaim,
each having excelled in their own way.

Whatever I call you, Lord,
however much I honor your name,
it can never be enough,
never even begin to express the homage you are due
for you are higher than my highest thoughts,
greater than the human mind can ever comprehend,
worthy of all praise and adoration.
Help me, today and always,
to worship you as you deserve.
Amen.

The Dinosaur Bones

They were ancient,
a reminder of life forms that walked the earth
not just centuries but eons ago—
for millions of years masters of all they surveyed—
the whole of human history, by comparison,
just a tiny speck,
a mere drop in the ocean.
Yet now they are gone,
the only clue to their existence a few fossil remains,
silent witness to a bygone age.

You alone, Lord, are eternal,
the same yesterday, today, and tomorrow.
You alone are before and beyond all,
the beginning and end of everything that is,
has been,
and shall be.
Yet you invite us,
seemingly here today and gone tomorrow—
like flowers fleetingly in bloom—
to share in eternity,
one with you forevermore.
For the breadth of your purpose
and wonder of your grace,
Lord, thank you.
Amen.

The Surveillance Cameras

It was a strange feeling,
reassuring yet also eerie,
for I was being watched,
my every move surveyed,
the all-seeing eye of the camera taking everything in
and storing it all away.

You, Lord, watch over me,
hour after hour,
day after day,
not to keep tabs on what I do,
but as a loving friend and faithful companion—
there to help in times of need,
protect in times of danger,
and comfort in times of hurt.
Thank you for the knowledge that,
though I lose sight of you,
still you look out for me.
Amen.

The Recorder Player

It was hardly a pleasant sound,
more of a shrill blast,
the child having little control of the instrument
and apparently even less musical sense,
yet she was enjoying herself,
letting loose with unbridled glee.

I want to make music for you, Lord,
to live my life as an exuberant melody of praise,
offered in gratitude for all you've done
and everything you'll always mean to me.
It may sometimes be out of tune,
more of a joyful noise than a work of art,
but receive it, I pray,
together with what I am and all I long to be,
for it comes from the heart,
with love.
Amen.

The Paint Palette

It was a stunning selection:
not just your run-of-the-mill colors
but every shade in between—
a diverse array of reds, yellows, blues, greens,
and innumerable others besides,
enough to paint almost any scene
and capture every nuance—
an artist's delight.

Yet for all its breadth, Lord,
that palette is as nothing compared to the one
you have used in creation,
its range of colors being magnified there
a million times over:
in the splendor of a sunset and magic of a rainbow,
the hues of the sea and glory of the sky,
the tints of autumn and tapestry of a garden,
the plumage of birds and loveliness of a meadow.
An immeasurable spectrum brightens every day,
causing me to catch my breath in wonder
and exult in spirit.
For the imprint of your hand on the canvas of life,
breathtaking beyond words,
receive my praise.
Amen.

The Tennis Court

The lines were clearly marked,
each of them integral to the court,
indicating whether the ball was long or short,
in or out.
They set the boundaries,
the confines of the game,
everything plain to all.

Lord, you set boundaries for me,
not to restrict or confine
but to give definition to who and what I am—
your love the space in which I live,
your guidance giving parameters to my life
and your mercy restoring me within them
when I step over the line.
For the meaning and direction I find in you,
receive my praise.
Amen.

The Pricked Finger

It was nothing,
just a tiny scratch
where the nail had pricked my finger,
but I sucked it ruefully,
feeling sorry for myself
if only for a moment.

But then, Lord, I remembered other nails,
thrust deep into hands and feet,
inflicting not just surface wounds,
but ripping through flesh and crushing bone,
the pain too dreadful to contemplate,
never mind the agony soon to follow.
For the immense love that could endure all this,
willingly,
gladly,
for one such as me,
receive my heartfelt praise.
Amen.

The Ream of Paper

It was a mess,
the page a mass of corrections,
not just one or two
but hundreds,
and the result was a shambles.
Yet no matter,
for I'd a ream of paper to work with—
not just one clean sheet,
but another . . .
and another . . .
and another . . .
as many, surely, as I could ever want.

Thank you, Lord, for the clean sheet you offer
when I make a mess of life;
your invitation to turn over a new leaf and start again.
Thank you that your mercy is never exhausted,
your patience never at an end;
that you go on offering new beginnings
for as many times as it takes.
Amen.

The Shopping Cart

She couldn't have managed without it,
the weight of shopping simply too much
for a woman of her years,
but the cart she pulled solved the problem,
bearing a load she could never have carried alone—
an impossible burden suddenly made light.

Thank you, Lord, that when I wrestle with heavy loads,
weighed down by problems that sap my strength
and troubles that crush the spirit,
you unfailingly come to my aid,
helping to shoulder
what I can no longer manage to bear.
Thank you for being there when I need you most,
ready to carry not only the burden
but me as well.
Amen.

The Hairdresser

What a strange job,
cutting all that hair,
head after head,
day after day.
Do they get bored? I wonder.
They must,
but they don't show it,
just make casual conversation as they snip away.
They're passing the time of day, of course,
for they don't know me,
not *really*—
don't know most of their customers, come to that.

But *you* do, Lord,
every hair of my head,
every thought of my mind,
every aspect of my character—
nothing hidden from your gaze.
Inside out and back to front,
you know each one of us,
and yearn that we might know you too.
For that great truth,
Lord, I praise you.
Amen.

The Space Probe

They were exciting pictures—
fascinating glimpses of swirling gas,
soaring mountains,
massive craters,
and rocky wastes.
At last we knew a little more about the universe beyond,
but it was simply a single planet,
one of trillions spiraling away into infinity;
in terms of our solar system,
let alone space,
just a stone's throw away.
For all it taught us,
the lesson brought home was how vast are the heavens
and how small is the earth.

Thank you, Lord, for the capacity of humankind
to explore profound mysteries,
for our ability constantly to push back the boundaries
of comprehension.
But thank you also for your incomparable greatness—
the unfathomable immensity of your love,
awesome breadth of your purpose,
and staggering scale of your power.
You are higher than our highest thoughts,
above all, before all, and beyond all.
Receive my praise.
Amen.

The Zoo

It was a snapshot, that's all,
a tiny insight into the awesome variety of creation,
the breathtaking diversity of life on earth—
animals, birds,
fish, reptiles,
insects, and so much more—
our visit that day offering a reminder
of the bewildering richness of it all,
the wonder of our world.

Thank you, Lord, for that special heritage,
so much to intrigue, entrance, fascinate, and amaze.
Teach me to appreciate
both the privilege and responsibility it represents,
not only rejoicing at all you have given
but also respecting its innate worth and dignity
and playing my part in protecting it for the future,
so that others may marvel in turn.
Amen.

The Sunglasses

They shielded my eyes from the worst of the glare,
allowing me to gaze for a moment at the setting sun
and glimpse its glory,
a golden ball of light.
Without them I was dazzled,
the light too much to bear,
forcing me to look away.

Before you also, Lord, I must turn aside,
your splendor too intense,
your brightness too awesome,
and yet, through Christ, I glimpse your grace and glory,
wonderful beyond words.
For now it is partial,
as though I look through darkened glasses,
but it is enough and more than enough
to lighten my path
and illuminate my soul.
Shine now,
shine always,
through his radiant love.
Amen.

The School Run

They waited to collect their children,
standing outside the classroom or at the gates
to meet them,
none willing to risk their little one's safety
by letting them walk home alone.
One day, perhaps,
but as long as their kids were vulnerable,
in need of support,
they'd continue to be there for them—
their welfare more important than anything.

Thank you, Lord, that *you* do not leave us alone,
instead drawing alongside us through your Spirit.
Thank you that,
just as you met with your followers on the road
and your disciples in the upper room,
so, in Christ, you meet with us on the journey of life,
always there, in your resurrection power,
to guide, protect, comfort, and support,
each of us valued as a little child,
chosen and precious to you.
Amen.

The River

It surged past me,
a mighty torrent,
and I marveled at the flow of water,
at how, year in, year out,
century after century,
despite days without rain,
even weeks of drought,
it never ran dry.

It spoke of you, Lord:
your faithful provision and constant love.
Through sunshine and storm,
summer or winter,
it remains the same—
a stream of living water,
refreshing and reviving,
unfailing,
come what may.
For the constancy of that provision,
receive my praise.
Amen.

The Symphony

The music stirred my heart,
bringing a lump to my throat;
the emotions it aroused so powerful,
almost overwhelming,
that my spirit soared with the melody,
transported to new heights:
an ecstasy beyond words.

May the same be true, Lord, of knowing you,
your presence causing me to catch my
breath in wonder,
to exult and marvel.
Instead of being an arid issue of the mind—
intellectually assenting to truth—
may faith be an affair of the heart,
capturing my imagination
and transporting me into your presence,
so that, overwhelmed with joy and filled with awe,
my spirit may rise to you each day
in rapturous praise and grateful worship.
Amen.

The Fountain

It danced in the breeze,
a cascade of water leaping and cavorting
like a newborn lamb,
a playful kitten—
exuberant,
free,
full of life.
Restless and vivacious,
it spoke of unquenchable energy,
an irrepressible vitality bubbling deep within.

May your Spirit, Lord, course through me
with similar energy,
your joy with comparable verve,
your love with equal spontaneity,
and your peace with matching abandon.
So fill me with your presence,
that my soul may dance each day
in jubilant praise and exultant gratitude.
Amen.

The Dawn Chorus

It was a wonderful sound:
a chorus of birdsong filling the still morning air,
exultant and ecstatic;
a jubilant psalm of praise to welcome the rising sun,
celebrating a new day after the long hours of darkness.

Thank you, Lord, for the new day you bring
through the rising of *your* Son,
the new beginnings,
new life,
you daily make possible through him.
Thank you for your promise that,
however deep the darkness may seem,
light will dawn again,
shining in our hearts forevermore.
Amen.

The Cockerel

It was an unfamiliar sound for a townsperson like me—
a cock crowing at the crack of dawn—
and for a moment I groaned in dismay,
eyes still heavy with sleep.
But then a shaft of sunlight flooded the room
and the sound of birdsong
drifted through the window—
reminders of another day,
new beginnings—
and I rose joyfully,
thankful for its promise.

Teach me, Lord, to greet each day with gratitude,
awakening with a sense of joy and expectation
at the possibilities of life.
Whatever fears I may have
or problems I may be facing,
help me to welcome the new morning as your gift
and to live every moment as fully as I am able.
Amen.

www.ingramcontent.com/pod-product-compliance
Lightning Source LLC
Chambersburg PA
CBHW052038070526
44584CB00020B/3153